OUTSTANDING IN HIS FIELD

by

The Rev. Steven R. Rottgers

Library of Congress Catalog Card Number: 95-68405

ISBN: 1-882792-10-6

Proctor Publications of Ann Arbor
Printed in the United States of America

Introduction and Acknowledgments

I am a believer that Life is a school where each day's class is provided with the appropriate teacher to aid us in adding our stitches to a tapestry of basic learned truths. The tapestry is presented to us from generations past so that we may add to it in preparation for passing it on to our children's generation.

I offer this parable as a thread that may enable you, the reader, to add your part to the continuous, woven fabric of life's tapestry. More important, I pray that you will lovingly pass it on to your child's generation for their learning and shared understanding.

Although countless threads have influenced my life, and ultimately made this book possible, I need to celebrate the loving influence of my family; Mr. & Mrs. Harry Rottgers, Mr.& Mrs. Stephen McVean, Mr.& Mrs. Robert Rottgers and my brother Robert, Mr. & Mrs. Carl Hassenstein & Peter.

I give thanks for those who taught and influenced my life in school and by their presence, especially the Rev.'s. Allen Person, David Heil, Wayne Yeager, Gregg Riley, Rodney Caulkins, and Capt. Wayne Larson of the Church Army, and the Rev. Joseph Grizone for his encouragement.

I rejoice in the supported friendship of this project by the CTKM; The Birds, Bunyards, Conways, Cooks, Eagen's, Gardener's, Haus's, Mabie's, Maces's, Miller's, Mize's, McClary's, Park's, Vermillion's and Polly Odam. I also wish to thank Hazel Proctor and her staff, The Rev. & Mrs. John Hagan, Mr. & Mrs. Tim Fox, Mr. & Mrs. Chuck Heilman, Sheila Watkins, Fran Pollard, Jo King, Ann Pearson, Mr. & Mrs. Dan Fletcher, Peter Bundarin & Ellen Thomas in memorial of John and Margaret Bundarin, and Scottie McNeil for their love and support.

Last, but certainly not least, I am humbled by the never-ending Love of my children Alex, Peter, and Molly, but especially by my greatest supporter, my wife Mary.

I thank the Great Master for all of these and more as we strive to become "Outstanding in HIS Field."

Steven R. Rottgers

For

Alex, Peter and Molly

And In Memory Of

Mr. Richard Palmer
Mrs. Betty Mace
Mr. Robert Conway

Canton was a scarecrow. How he became a scarecrow, he didn't know, his creation avoided this knowledge just as birth resists human memory. His earliest memory was only of a farmer, Mr. Palmer, placing a broad brimmed hat on his yellow straw toupee. It looked nice on top of his burlap sack head. It actually brought his personality to life.

The first words heard by the scarecrow were also those of Mr. Palmer saying, "Canton, that's a good name for you. Your hat band will let everyone know exactly who you are." Sure enough, Canton quickly became known personally by all who drove down Warren Road by the Palmer Farm. They saw the red hat band; a remnant scrap from a feed sack advertising the Canton Seed and Farm Supply Store. The word Canton banded his brow for all to see.

He was clothed in a red polka-dot shirt, blue jean pants with a rope belt. Two shoes were tacked to the stakes that supported him as legs. The cross piece that traversed his shoulders ended in stick-fashioned hands.

Two large black button eyes and a conical nose fashioned from a twine spindle gave expression to Canton's burlap face. His mouth, sewn in a frown to frighten away pest, had been the opening for stuffing his head when Canton was assembled.

He was a grand scarecrow!

Mr. Palmer's parting words were, "Watch over the field, Canton. It's in your care now." He then left the field where Canton stood sentinel.

Canton felt important! He was in charge now! As he looked far and wide to survey his turf, he

was dismayed to only see rows of small green sprouts. His field was nothing more than fuzzy green rows that formed a green blanket. It totally surrounded him, for as far as he could see. His pride sank, but only for a moment. At least it was *his* fuzzy green blanket. He would still take care of it because it was *his*. He was standing in the middle of *his* green kingdom.

As the weeks passed by, Canton's pride and feelings of success were only fueled by his awareness that *his* fuzzy green field was getting deeper, thicker and greener. He stood tall to survey all that he had. It had been worth withstanding the Spring rains and the hot rays of the early Summer sun. The evidence surrounded him, like a deep lush carpet of green.

One bright morning, Canton became aware of movement at the edge of the field that bordered the forest. He could only see out of the corner of his eyes but something was there. Fear gave way to panic. "Get away from my field!" said Canton in a stern voice to cover his own fear. No answer. "I said, get out of my field!" Canton's anger rose to the silent challenge of his ownership.

The heads of five young rabbits and their mother slowly rose above the blades of the green plants. "Oh, dear scarecrow," said the mother rabbit, "We've come from our burrow to allow the children their first sweet taste of green plants. I've never seen such a large and green field before. Please, there is so much and we need so little, let us have just a sampling of your field and we will travel on."

"No!" bellowed Canton, "It's mine and I'm taking care of all of it. You must leave now and stop eating immediately!" Slowly their heads were lowered and each rabbit followed its mother back to the forest.

Canton felt good. He had done his job. He'd show any other animal from the forest just who was in charge, just as he'd shown the rabbits. The message was out amongst the animals. Many had tried and yet were scared off by Canton.

With the coming of the long summer heat that stifled and browned the edge of the field, Canton's zeal grew even stronger to protect all that was his. He would not even relinquish the stunted plants to the parched hungers of the local raccoons, rabbits, squirrels or field mice. *It was all his!*

The heat of the Summer, the heavy rains of humid afternoons and just the passing of time brought changes to Canton's world.

The short, fuzzy green blanket of Spring was now chest-high to Canton and there were budding ears of sweet corn on each plant. Canton strained with pride to look over the tops of a sea of green and gold tassels. It was a good field to be in charge of, and with such potential, Canton felt grand.

The other change was inside Canton. The stakes and timbers that kept Canton erect were becoming a bother. He frequently cursed their rigidity and the discomfort they caused him from the base of his spine to the cross-members through his shoulders. They tormented him more and more as he tried to defend his field from would-be trespassers. It seemed that the very timbers that served as a throne to survey his kingdom, also were the stumbling block to his will to control it. They rendered him immobile and with an ever-increasing irritability in the very field he loved.

The waning of Summer brought a burst of gold and silver from the ears of corn on each plant. Harvest time was nearing. The gathering of the fruits of Canton's hard labor was close at hand. Mr.

Palmer would be pleased, and Canton was bursting with pride.

Winds, hinting of the change of season, brought evidence that the harvest was soon. Flying by, as if one with the breeze, a lone dove came to alight on Canton's shoulder and asked permission to rest. "Thank you for letting me catch my breath!" said the dove. "My name is Meta. It is a nickname for a longer version that my mother gave me. She said that I always seem to be around when something new or changing is taking place."

"I'm glad to meet you, Meta," said Canton. "The only change coming soon will be the harvest. Is that why you're here?"

"I don't know! Maybe," replied Meta. She admired the field. "It's a very nice field."

"Yes it is, and it's all mine!" gloated Canton.

Meta looked deep into Canton's eyes and said, "You must be Canton the scarecrow. I've heard of you. You're a very proud and fierce scarecrow who shares nothing from his field. Word of you has traveled far and wide in the animal kingdom." Canton's ego inflated a bit more. Meta continued, "Don't let your pride and wealth of this field blind you of things that are greater. Thank you for the resting spot. I must be off, but I'll be back to visit again someday."

She was gone with the next breeze and out of sight before Canton could reply, "There is nothing greater than my field!"

Sure enough, Meta knew something that Canton knew nothing about. The animals all talked about the scarecrow who shared nothing and reigned over his field with the fierceness of a tyrant. What

could they do? Even the feeding of their young was a problem. During the dryness of the late Summer, much of the low forest plants had dried up and Canton's field was the closest and largest source of food available to them.

A large band of nature's mischief-makers rose to the challenge and claimed that they would put the scarecrow to the test. They would raid his field. The crows, however, did not tell the other animals of their real intent, which was to take all the corn for themselves.

"Caw, caw," the cry rose up and in moments a few crows became an army of thousands. They flew as a dark cloud toward Canton's field.

Canton was enjoying a midday nap from his sentry post when he was awakened by the rustle of wings and the constant war cries of "Caw, caw." A black cloud of crows engulfed Canton's field of green in their blackness.

What later became known by animals all over the forest as the "Battle of the Greediest of Greedies" had begun.

"Go!"

"Caw."

"Get out of here!"

"Caw, caw."

"This is *my* field!"

"Caw."

"Go away!"

"Caw, caw."

"Don't do that!"

"Caw" rose from the field in echo-fashion and gave evidence of a heated battle of wills, spirits and turf.

Canton strained with all of his might against the timbers throughout his body in hopes of some freedom and movement to scare the invaders away. The only movement afforded by his efforts was the lowering of one hand which equally raised the other. It was a moment of false security. Canton thought that he could now stop those low to the ground and high in the air. His hope disappeared into fear, grief and horror as another black cloud of reinforcements arrived over the trees.

With lightning speed, an army who were experts at greed, waste and robbery laid waste to the once lush cornfield and left it as rubble around Canton's feet. The victors, filled with their spoils, left the field of battle. Some flew, some waddled, some fell into engorged sleep. A squad was left to mop up the leftovers.

Lucifer, the head crow, couldn't resist the urge to taunt the demoralized scarecrow. Pacing back and forth on the canted shoulders of Canton, he took beak-filled bites of straw from his hat. As he paced by, Lucifer barbed his statements for Canton's ears, "That sure was an outstanding field! It tasted so good! I'm glad you took such good care of it. We didn't miss a morsel! Now, what are you going to do when Mr. Palmer comes back? Some scarecrow you are! You failed; you'll be dismantled. You have

already started to fall apart. Look how your shoulders slope! You can't be Canton, the great scarecrow! You're broken and can scare nothing! Your name should be Canted, not Canton!" With these parting shots to Canton's heart, Lucifer and the remnant band left Canton to a cold, dark night and his desolate field.

Despite the full load of stuffing that gave Canton form, he felt hollow inside. There was nothing there, no feelings except for pain and the grief that accompanies loss. As the night crept on, rage and revengeful anger seethed within him. His misery was multiplied and festered by the ever present splinters which surfaced his rigid spine and shoulder crosspiece. He'd show the crows and all the animals next year!

Even this dream of revenge evaporated with the morning frost. He awoke to Mr. Palmer's words as he viewed the field's carnage at a distance. "I guess I need to replace you, Canton. You were doing so well. What happened? I can't risk another total loss next year. Maybe if I fixed you into a different style? Anyway, I'll wait until next Spring, after the Winter. You and I will have to think about it for a while." Mr. Palmer slowly walked away and Canton's dream of revenge withered away with his last ray of hope.

It was over! He'd be replaced with no second chance, just the stark reality of facing stubble remnants that were ghostly reminders of a dream lost and unrecoverable.

Nights became colder and longer. The winds blew louder and cut with a knife's sharpness, they honed the edge of Canton's bitterness.

One blustery morning, Canton awoke to a familiar voice. "What has happened here!?" It was

Meta, trying to maintain her balance against the wind and still perch on Canton's sloping shoulder.

"I lost it all to an army of crows and became broken in the battle. Mr. Palmer wants to replace or change me next year, that's all!" fired Canton. "During your last visit you said that change usually occurs when you are around. Didn't you over do it a bit!? Are you happy now? So, are you through with me and can now move on to some other poor scarecrow, or where ever you go, to change them!? Maybe you returned to finish me off!"

Meta patiently weathered Canton's storm of words and calmly replied, "I only came to visit you and assure you of my love. I don't cause or choose the change that usually happens when I visit somewhere or someone. The change that happens often comes from inside of whomever I meet, not from the outside. You are looking for someone to blame. It looks like the change in your life is not complete but hopefully is just starting. Remember, Canton, there is something greater than us controlling all things, and the boundaries of life expand beyond fields and wealth or self pride. Take these seeds for new thoughts. A new life comes with the change that will grow in you if they are planted well. You'll see a new harvest."

She was gone with the next gust of wind that accompanied Canton's "Humph!" The only harvest he had seen was the gathering of the strewn corn stalks that had dried to a dead brown and were being used by the local families as decorations for Halloween and Thanksgiving. "Some harvest!" thought Canton.

Halloween night was the celebration night for all scarecrows to joyously close the harvest gather-

ing season for another year. It re-stirred Canton's painful memories of his field, the forest animals, the crows, Mr. Palmer's disappointment and Meta's parting words. He heard from voices carried on the silence of the moonlit night, stories and songs about the Great Master's approval of the other scare-crows' seasonal work.

"Who was this Great Master?" thought Canton. "How do you get His approval?"

"It doesn't matter," replied Canton's thoughts. "You won't meet Him because you have nothing to give Him anyway. Why would He even think that He had any right to the harvest? It's my field anyway! He didn't even help protect it when it was under attack! If He'd come to *my* field, I'd show Him!"

Canton went to sleep early that night.

The next day was filled with turbulent weather changes. Canton almost expected a visit from Meta but she never appeared. The day and its wet, blustery greyness gave way to the darkness. It was the scariest night that Canton had ever experienced. A violent thunderstorm hung over Mr. Palmer's farm.

Canton was being shaken to his wooden core and feared that he would be blown away, uprooted entirely by the force of the gusting wind. The gust were not glancing blows but full frontal assaults on Canton's whole frame. Rain pelted his face and brow while flashes of lightning and the resultant boom of thunder humbled the scarecrow to a realization that he was so small and lost in a storm of loneliness. "I am so sorry!" cried Canton. "I wish I could do it over again!" The rain formed tears that streamed down his face.

A thunderous roar resounded the heavens as if formed by the clapping of the Great Master's hands Himself. The sparked bolt of lightning struck the very heart of Canton's chest and broke the rigid joint where his shoulder and wooden spine were joined. Canton sighed, "I am truly broken now."

He felt himself sag on the same stakes that used to hold him so proudly, but also caused a source of his pain.

The wind continued to blow and tilted Canton's head back into a gaze toward the heavens. His hat was blown free and was swept into the night. He was finally arrested in his descent to a humble bow when the weight of his body pulled the broken crosspieces of his arms upward to sustain him, as if reaching for the sky.

The tarpaulin that covered a nearby haystack tore loose and shrouded itself over Canton's head and body. Finally the wind stilled as the thunder and lightning abated. Rain fell in a constant saturating flow as if attempting to cleanse away the pain and memories of the past. Canton hung motionless, gazing upward as the rain bathed his face with a calmness that Canton had never felt before.

He fell into a deep, peaceful sleep that lasted the whole next day, and the day after that.

It was the soft voice of Meta whispering into Canton's ear that gently woke him. "Wake up Canton! You look so different! Are you allright?"

"Yes" replied Canton, "I'm fine." The words came out so easily and without the usual muffled sound. Canton was no longer muted by the stitches of his mouth. The rain-soaked stitches had given way and allowed his mouth to open into a tremendous radiant smile of gold straw stuffing. The horrible

frown that Canton had always worn was now a beaming expression of joy.

"Meta," said Canton, "I have changed! It all started when I heard of someone called the Great Master on Halloween Night. I truly felt sad that I had nothing to offer Him from the harvest of this field. I wished that I could start over and try again. I could be a much better scarecrow. I know now that this field is the Great Master's and Mr. Palmer only wanted me to care for it, not own it. I could have shared some of it with the animals and made some friends. There would have been plenty left after their gleaning. I tried to keep all of it for myself and lost every bit of it before the harvest. Meta, will I ever be able to meet the Great Master and maybe give Him some of this field's harvest?" he asked.

After surveying Canton's new denim vestment and his new posture, she spoke in his ear, "He was here that night and you gave Him the most precious harvest any scarecrow could offer, his selfish pride. There are many scarecrows, in many fields, on many farms, who forget that they are caretakers, not landowners. Their pride and thoughts of ownership blinds them from the need for a gentle, yet wise life of the caretaker. Their pride may award them quick success, but eventually, they are challenged with the same lesson you faced. It could be drought, or flood, worm or crow, but somehow, someone will deliver the message. The greatest test is: will the scarecrow listen and learn? I'm glad you did, Canton!"

"Do you think the Great Master knows that I've changed?" asked Canton.

"Oh yes," replied Meta.

"Will I get another chance?" questioned Canton.

"That's for the Great Master, Mr. Palmer, and you to answer at the right time," mused Meta.

"You'll know the answer soon, Canton. There are other fields to visit but I'll be back to visit in the Spring."

"Goodbye," said Canton. "I do thank you for your help and look forward to our next visit."

Meta flew out of sight, amid the first flurries of snow riding the North Wind.

The passage of time for Canton slowed with the expectant hope of meeting the Great Master and finding out what would be his destiny.

As the next few weeks passed, Canton's new outlook and heavenly gaze brought a whole different world into view. Canton occupied himself by watching the clouds play chase across the sky, catching snowflakes in his open mouth or exchanging greetings with the formations of geese heading South to warmer climates. The sun was so bright, so round. The moon changed it's face each night and silhouetted grey ghostlike clouds that continued their daytime cousin's game of chase.

The one act of this heavenly showcase that filled Canton with awe and wonder was the forever-depth and beauty of a clear still night and the glory of the shining stars. This sight seemed to stir prayerful questions for Canton. He addressed them to the Great Master. How he hoped they would be answered soon. Canton's gaze wandered the starlit sky as if looking for the answer and always focused ultimately on one particular star for no apparent reason. It did, however, serve as the ending punctuation mark for each session.

And so it was until one similar session on a starlit night in December. A blanket of snow hushed any unnecessary distractions and gave luminous reflection of the stars and moon. "Are you really there!?

Will there be an answer?" sighed Canton. As the words rose to the stars, Canton became aware of sing-ing voices flowing from the village. Shortly after the fading of the sweet melody, a car came down the road and stopped in front of Canton's field. It was Mr. and Mrs. Palmer, dressed in their finest clothes. They carefully made their way to the fence line. Canton felt their eyes looking at him. He strained to quell the shaking he could feel, not from the cold, but from the expectations of what might happen.

Then Canton heard Mr. Palmer's voice, "You know, I was sure that I was going to replace that scarecrow, but after seeing him now, especially tonight, I think he deserves another chance. Honey, he even looks different, as if directing everyone's attention to things more important. It's like he is praying for the success of the field to someone greater than himself. He seems to have learned a lesson from the past year. You deserve another season, Canton. We'll try again in the Spring." The Palmers drove off.

"Oh, thank you, thank you!" said Canton with joyful praise. "You really are there! You really did hear me! I will always remember that this is your field and I will take good care of it. I will share with those in need that you send to me and maybe they will help me ward off the greedy trespassers." Canton's gaze, by habit, focused like a period on the lone star for punctuation. It burst in affirmation, glory and radiance as if to signify receipt of the prayer. The star continued to radiate its beauty through-out the night. It bathed the scarecrow with hope and a sense of truly being loved.

From that day on, Mr. Palmer's farm yielded a full harvest of sweetcorn, enough to feed residents of the towns and villages surrounding Canton. The local forest animals had plenty to eat and aided him whenever needed. Meta also visited Canton regularly which spirited a lasting relationship.

Local residents didn't understand how all of this came to be, but it seemed to have something to do with the scarecrow praying in Mr. Palmer's field. He looked like Canton, but was different. A new name began to circulate among those who passed by the Palmer Farm. Children and adults would all hail greetings to Canton, the Praying Scarecrow, as they drove by on Warren Road.

It made Canton glad to have so many friends and he smiled at each of their greetings, but he never moved his eyes from his prayerful gaze upward to the Great Master.

Canton was a grand scarecrow!
He was outstanding in *HIS* field.

THE END